GROWING
FLOWERS

Tracy Nelson Maurer

The Rourke Book Company, Inc.
Vero Beach, Florida 32964

Tracy Nelson Maurer specializes in nonfiction and business writing. Her most recently published children's books include the Bodyworks series, also from Rourke Publishing. A graduate of the University of Minnesota Journalism School, Tracy lives with her husband Mike and two children in Superior, Wisconsin.

With appreciation to gardeners Lois M. Nelson, Harvey Almstedt, and Lois I. Nelson; and to Richard J. Zondag, Jung Seed Company.

PHOTO CREDITS:
All photos and illustrations © East Coast Studios except p. 4 © David and Patricia Armentrout; p. 10, © USDA

PRODUCED & DESIGNED by East Coast Studios
eastcoaststudios.com

EDITORIAL SERVICES:
Lois M. Nelson
Pamela Schroeder

Library of Congress Cataloging-in-Publication Data

Maurer, Tracy, 1965-
   Growing flowers / Tracy Nelson Maurer.
     p. cm. — (Green thumb guides)
   Includes bibliographical references (p.).
   Summary: Describes how to choose, plant, and care for various kinds of flowers.
   ISBN 1-55916-251-1
   1. Flower gardening—Juvenile literature. 2. Flowers—Juvenile literature. [1. Flower gardening. 2. Gardening.]
I. Title.

SB406.5 .M38 2000
635.9—dc21

00–026923

Printed in the USA

Table of Contents

Why Grow Flowers?

People plant flowers for many reasons. Flowers add colors, smells, and shapes to the world.

Some gardeners grow flowers for **bouquets** (boh KAYZ) or just to look at them sway in the breeze.

Other gardeners grow flowers to feed butterflies, bees, and birds. These flying friends find food, called nectar, inside flowers. Hummingbirds especially like to sip nectar from trumpet-shaped flowers, such as petunias and morning glories.

Fun Fact

Scientists give every plant a Latin name. When you see a "daisy," scientists see a *Bellis perennis*.

Children and adults enjoy growing flowers. This dog seems to like how the flowers smell!

Pick the Right Flowers

Do you want to plant **perennials** (puh REN ee ulz) or **annuals** (AN you ulz), or both, in your garden?

Perennials need very little care. They come back every year. Green parts above ground die in the fall. Then they grow again in the spring. Perennials usually bloom for just a few weeks. Some bloom for only a few days.

Tulips are perennials that grow from bulbs every spring.

Sunflowers are annuals that grow quickly. They make pretty bouquets. People, birds, and animals eat sunflower seeds.

Most annuals bloom all **season** (SEE zon), much longer than perennials. These flowers don't come back in the spring. You must plant them every year. "Annual" means "year."

Easy Flowers to Grow

Perennials	Annuals
1. Tulip	1. Sunflower
2. Daisy	2. Marigold
3. Lily	3. Petunia
4. Mum	4. Alyssum
5. Hosta	5. Cosmo

Follow the Sun

Plants need soil, water, air, and sun to grow. Some flowers like more sunshine than others. Young sunflowers face the sun, turning from east to west during the day.

Some flowers like shade. Impatiens (im PAY shi enz) add bright colors to dim places.

Before you plant flowers, draw a sun map of your garden. Watch the garden all day. Mark on your map where the sun shines the most. Mark where it shines the least.

This sun map shows the sunny places in the yard. It also shows the shadows from the house and trees. The shadows move from east to west during the day.

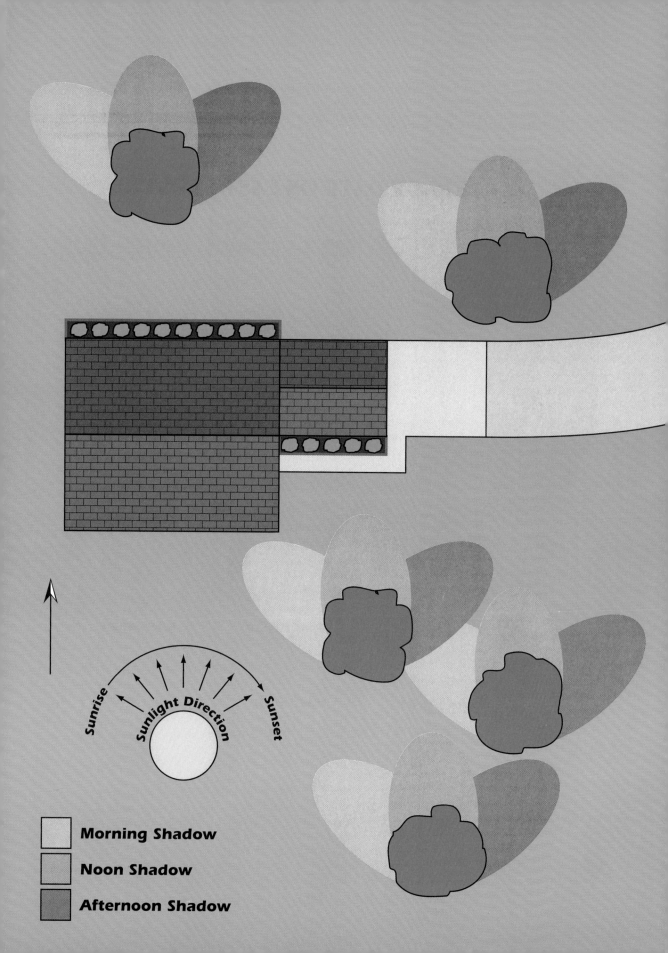

Morning Shadow

Noon Shadow

Afternoon Shadow

Sunrise

Sunlight Direction

Sunset

AVERAGE DATE OF LAST FROST

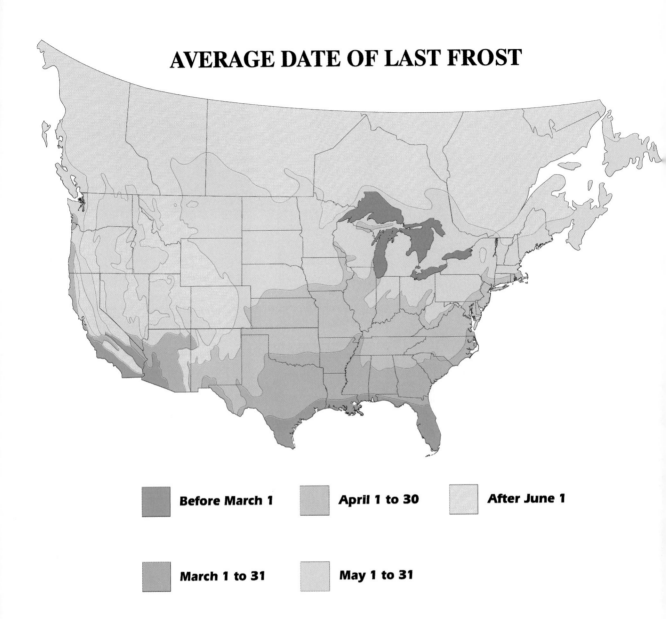

■ Before March 1	■ April 1 to 30	■ After June 1
■ March 1 to 31	■ May 1 to 31	

Planting Zones

Weather affects how your flowers grow. Gardeners check a Plant Hardiness Zone Map before they choose plants. The U.S. Department of Agriculture makes the official zone map. You can find many others like it in gardening books, such as the zone map here.

Gardeners wait to plant until after the last spring frost. A zone map shows when frosts usually stop for each part of the country.

A zone map also helps gardeners know which flowers grow best where they live. For example, pansies wilt in the summer heat of southern zones. They like the cooler summers in northern zones.

A zone map like this one helps gardeners know when to plant their flowers. Where do you live? When should you plant in your zone?

The Planting Plan

Before you plant outdoors, draw circles on your sun map where you want to plant flowers. Leave room to water and weed the flowers.

Look at your plant's seed packet or small plastic stick in its pot. A small sun means the plant grows in full sunshine. A circle cut in half means it likes some shade. A dark circle tells you to plant it in full shade. Check your sun map.

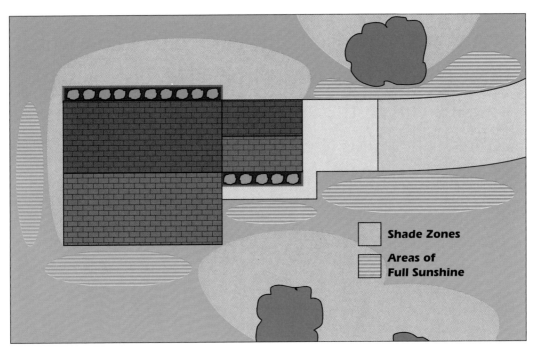

Shade Zones

Areas of
Full Sunshine

Using your sun map (page 9), draw circles to show where you would plant in full sun or shade.

Look at the package to learn how to plant your seeds. This package shows that the squash will grow best in full sun.

Plant smaller flowers in front of bigger flowers. You'll want to see them all!

Planting Ideas

Try a "Butterfly Garden." Butterflies like zinnias, cosmos, clover, and many other flowers. Or "paint" your garden with flowers of the same color.

The Dirt on Dirt

Dirt isn't just dirt to gardeners. It's soil. Flowers grow best in soil called loam. Loam has large and small pieces of earth mixed with **organic matter** (or GAN ick MAT ur). Water seeps easily through loam to the roots.

New gardens often have clay or sand instead of loam. Clay starves plant roots of water and air. Sand lets in too much air and the water sinks away. Adding organic matter to clay or sand helps flowers grow.

Gardening Tools

Rake: Clean and mix soil.
Hoe: Chop clumpy soil.
Trowel: Dig small holes for little plants.
Shovel: Dig big holes for big plants.
Bucket: Carry old plants away or fill for watering.
Gloves: Protect hands from scratches.

Loam helps bring food, water, and air to the plant roots. It looks like chocolate cake crumbs in your hand.

Sowing Seeds

Planting seeds usually costs less than buying plants at a **nursery** (NUR sur ee). Gardeners think it's fun to see a seedling sprout from the soil.

Look on the back of the seed package to learn how to plant, or sow, the seeds. Stick your finger into the soil to make a hole. Drop in one seed. Fill the hole with soil and pat it. Water the seed. Keep it moist for the next few weeks. Wait to see what happens!

Fun Fact

Sometimes seeds plant themselves in the spring. These "volunteers" come from last season's flowers. Birds or the wind carries the seeds to good soil.

Read the package to learn how deep to plant your seeds. Many seeds grow best in holes about 1/4" deep. Other seeds sprout with a thin layer of soil covering them.

Tending Your Garden

Tending, or taking care of, flowers makes gardeners happy. They like the fresh air and quiet.

Gardeners make sure their plants get enough water. Most outdoor gardens need about 1 inch (2.5 centimeters) of water each week.

Plants need water to grow. Try not to pour water on top of the plant. Aim for the ground under the leaves.

Pull weeds as soon as you see them. Too many weeds in your garden will keep your flowers from growing well.

Gardeners must also pull out weeds. Weeds are any plants that don't belong in the garden. Weeds steal water and soil **nutrients** (NEW tree ents) from your flowers. If you let weeds stay, they make seeds, too. Soon even more weeds will grow and hurt your flowers!

Blooms to Share

Share your flowers and watch your friendships bloom! At least, that's what gardeners think. Some flowers have special meanings. Red roses say, "I love you." Gardeners also share seeds and whole plants.

People enjoy flowers at the dinner table, too. Geranium petals spice up salads. Dandelions make a tasty wine. Sunflower seeds taste like nuts. Always check with an adult before eating any flowers.

Happy gardening!

Gardeners like to share their pretty flowers. This yellow mum in a pot will look cheery in her home.

GLOSSARY

annuals (AN you ulz) — plants that grow for one season and die in the fall

bouquets (boh KAYZ) — bunches of flowers

nursery (NUR sur ee) — a place where plants are grown and sold

nutrients (NEW tree ents) — food for energy to grow

organic matter (or GAN ick MAT ur) — well-rotted pieces from anything that once was alive, such as old leaves, cow manure, or fish bones

perennials (puh REN ee ulz) — plants with green parts that die in the fall; the green parts grow back again from the roots in the spring

season (SEE zon) — for plants, the time of year when the weather allows them to grow

These children are planting flowers near their school. You can plant flowers just about anywhere—in flowerbeds outdoors or in pots indoors.

INDEX

FURTHER READING

Find out more about gardening with these helpful books:

• Ambler, Wayne et al. *Treasury of Gardening.* Lincolnwood, Ill.: Publications International, 1994.

• Hart, Avery, and Paul Mantell. *Kids Garden!: The Anytime, Anyplace Guide To Sowing & Growing Fun.* Charlotte, Vermont: Williamson Publishing Co., 1996.

• Pohl, Kathleen. *Sunflowers.* Milwaukee: Raintree Publishers, 1997.

• *Rodale's Illustrated Encyclopedia of Gardening and Landscaping Techniques.* Edited by Barbara W. Ellis. Emmaus, Penn.: Rodale Press, 1990.

On-line resources:

Search for "kids gardening" on the World Wide Web to see many different sites.

• www.garden.org (c) National Gardening Association, 1999.